Desert Food Chains

By Julia Vogel

Illustrated by Hazel Adams

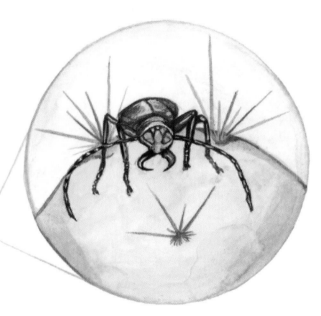

Content Consultant
Charles A. S. Hall, PhD
Professor of Environmental and Forest Biology
State University of New York
College of Environmental Sciences and Forestry

visit us at www.abdopublishing.com

Printed in the United States of America, North Mankato, Minnesota.
042010
092010
 THIS BOOK CONTAINS AT LEAST 10% RECYCLED MATERIALS.

Text by Julia Vogel
Illustrations by Hazel Adams
Edited by Nadia Higgins
Interior layout and design by Nicole Brecke
Cover design by Kazuko Collins

Library of Congress Cataloging-in-Publication Data
Vogel, Julia.
  Desert food chains / by Julia Vogel ; illustrated by Hazel Adams.
      p. cm. — (Fascinating food chains)
  Includes index.
  ISBN 978-1-60270-794-8
  1. Desert ecology—Juvenile literature. 2. Food chains (Ecology)—Juvenile literature. I. Adams, Hazel, 1983- ill. II. Title.
  QH541.5.D4V637 2011
  577.54'16—dc22
                          2009050527

Table of Contents

A Desert Food Chain

A food chain helps explain who eats what. It shows how living things need each other. Let's find out what's for dinner in the desert!

In one desert food chain, cactus seeds come first. A kangaroo rat gobbles them up. But the little, furry animal is also good to eat. A rattlesnake swallows the kangaroo rat whole. Then a hungry coyote is on the prowl. Snap! The fierce coyote attacks the rattlesnake.

Seeds to rat to snake to coyote. That's a simple food chain. But then a jackrabbit comes along and also feasts on cactus seeds. Another food chain begins. When many food chains connect, they make food webs.

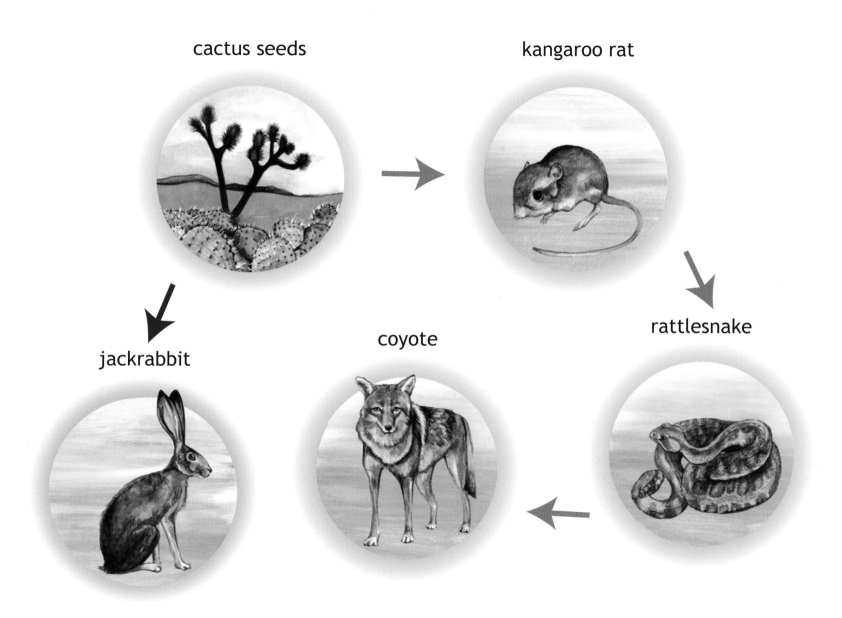

cactus seeds

kangaroo rat

jackrabbit

coyote

rattlesnake

Food provides the energy and the nutrients that living things need to stay alive. The arrows show which way food's nutrients and energy move through a desert food chain.

Dry as a Desert

A desert is one of the driest places on Earth. It hardly ever rains there. The hot sun beats down on sand and rocks. And yet, many animals and plants live in this harsh world. Their amazing food chains help them survive.

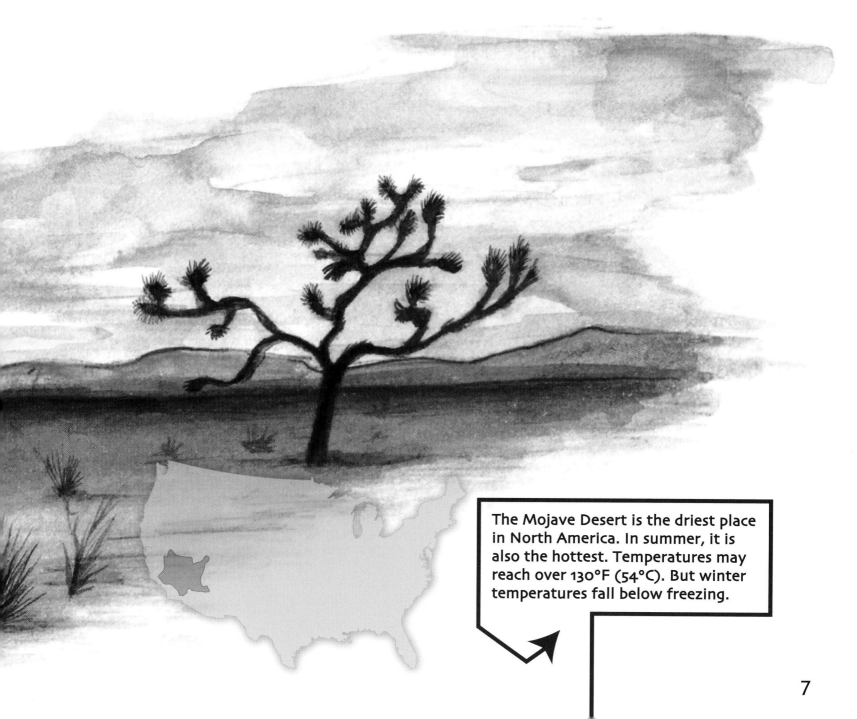

The Mojave Desert is the driest place in North America. In summer, it is also the hottest. Temperatures may reach over 130°F (54°C). But winter temperatures fall below freezing.

Plants Come First

Cacti and other plants are at the bottom of a desert food chain. They don't eat any living things. Instead, they live off sunlight and water. In the desert, there's plenty of sunshine. But how do plants get enough water?

Special traits help desert plants live with little rain. Their tough skins keep water in. Their roots slurp up every raindrop they can reach.

A barrel cactus has deep folds in its stem. When the rains come, the folds expand. The plant swells, storing extra water to use later.

Herbivores Eat Plants

A cactus beetle has super strong jaws. It can bite through the thick skin of a cactus. A jackrabbit's sharp teeth can nibble around prickly cactus thorns. These animals are herbivores. They eat plants. They are the next link in the food chain.

A chuckwalla munches leaves but never takes a sip of water. The lizard gets all the water it needs from plants.

The sun sets over the sand dunes. The desert cools. Now is the time when many herbivores come out to find food. Mule deer walk down from the hills to eat grass. Kangaroo rats leave underground nests to gather cactus seeds. They are nocturnal animals.

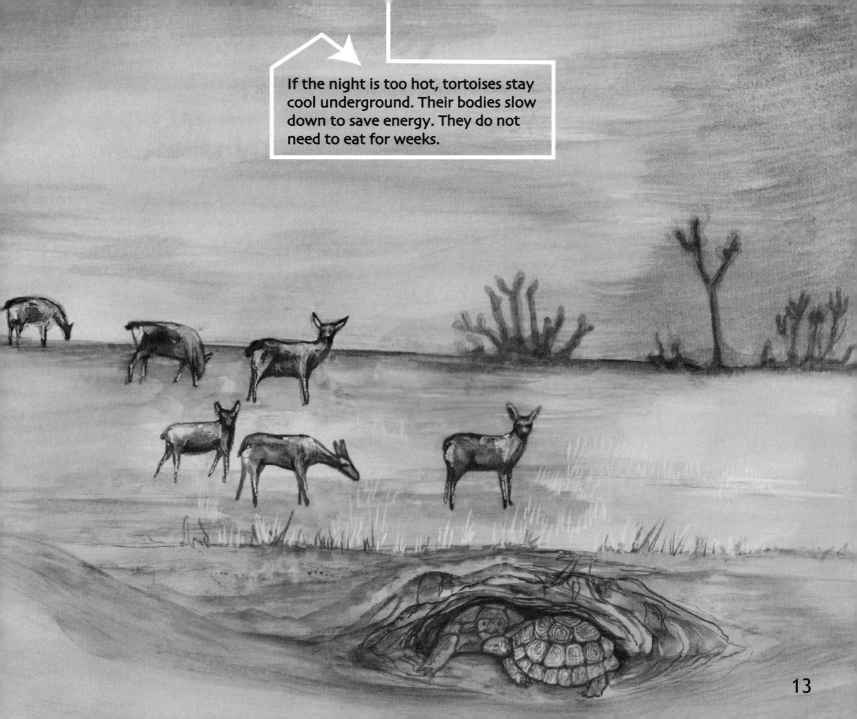

13

Carnivores Eat Meat

A rattlesnake is also nocturnal. It waits behind a rock. When a kangaroo rat hops by, the snake strikes. It swallows the rat whole. Nutrients and energy from seeds the rat ate end up inside the snake.

Animals that eat other animals are called carnivores. They are the next food chain link.

Snakes, spiders, and other desert predators often kill their prey with venom. A scorpion in Africa's Sahara Desert has a sting that can kill a human.

Top Carnivores Rule

The rattlesnake is full from the meat it ate. But it had better not rest. Along comes a red-tailed hawk. The fierce bird grabs the snake.

The hawk is a top carnivore. It hunts other meat eaters, like the snake. Top carnivores, such as hawks and bobcats, rule the food chain. Usually, nothing dares eat these large, powerful animals.

Omnivores Have Lots of Choices

A coyote can pounce on a rattlesnake or dig up a tortoise nest. It can gobble fruit from prickly pears or Joshua trees. Animals that eat both plants and animals are called omnivores. They find lots of food in the desert.

Decomposers Clean Up

A coyote will also eat a dead deer. It eats its fill and wanders off. Worms, larvae, and tiny bacteria also come out to feed on the leftovers. These decomposers break down bones and meat. They also feed on rotting plants and animal waste.

Decomposers clean up the desert. As they do, they put nutrients back into the soil. This helps plants grow.

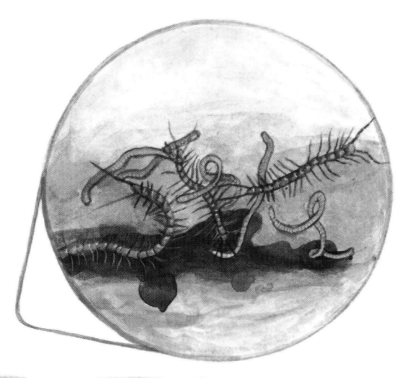

Decomposers can also be food for animals. Millipedes are decomposers that feed on dead cacti. These creatures are also hunted by tarantula spiders.

Rain at Last

After many dry months, clouds darken the sky. Rain pours down. In a few days, plants sprout and bloom. Tortoises come out to eat new leaves. Hummingbirds sip sweet nectar from bright flowers everywhere.

Carnivores feast, too. Toads snatch flies. The toads lay eggs in new ponds. Their tadpoles must grow quickly before the ponds dry up again.

Winter is the rainy season in the Mojave Desert. Most of the year's rain may fall in a few days. Dried up rivers fill up and often flood.

People and the Food Chain

Long ago, American Indians ate cactus fruit and other plants in the Mojave Desert. They hunted bighorn sheep, jackrabbits, and lizards. People today can still be part of the desert food chain. However, to find food, they must know the desert well.

Today, people use the desert in many ways. Ranchers graze cattle. Farmers grow crops. Cities take over land.

Cattle, crops, and cities take up space where wild plants and animals used to live. They use up water, too. They can hurt desert food chains. If one link in a food chain goes away, so could the other links that depend on it.

People go to the desert to have fun. Some ride motorbikes across the sands. They may not realize their bikes can harm the desert's plants— and the rest of the food chain.

Deserts are easily damaged, and they take a long time to heal. But you can help protect desert food chains.

Don't waste water when you shower. Never dump harmful chemicals down the drain. Most important, learn as much as you can about deserts. Tell other people how important and interesting deserts and their food chains are!

Some fish and other animals and plants in the Mojave could die out. If that happens, the food chain may weaken.

Food Chain Science

Scientists often study desert food chains and food webs. They want to learn about all the ways plants and animals are connected. During their research, they discovered that tortoises are disappearing from the Mojave Desert. Scientists studied what was hurting tortoises. They found that many of them get hit by cars. Also, cattle graze on the plants tortoises eat.

Another threat to tortoises took researchers by surprise. They discovered baby tortoise shells near raven nests. The birds were feeding baby tortoises to their young.

Scientists counted more and more shells every year. So, they counted the ravens. There were more of the birds than ever in the Mojave. Their flocks are growing because they are eating garbage people toss outside.

Scientists saw a new way to protect tortoises by reducing raven numbers. They began teaching people to keep garbage away from ravens. By studying food webs, scientists learn how to protect animals and plants in deserts and around the world.

Fun Facts

Deserts are always dry, but they're not always hot. Antarctica is technically Earth's largest desert. The largest hot desert on Earth is the Sahara, which covers most of North Africa.

There are four deserts in North America: the Mojave, the Chihuahua, the Sonora, and the Great Basin. The driest, hottest place in North America is Death Valley in the Mojave Desert.

An oasis is a place in the desert that has water all the time. It is often where a spring bubbles up. In the Mojave, the Mara Oasis is a cool place for palm trees and many other plants and animals not found in other parts of the desert.

Camels may be the most famous desert animals. Fatty humps on their backs and other traits allow them to travel for days without eating or drinking.

Gila monsters are large, brightly patterned lizards. People fear their poisonous bites, but Gila monsters spend most of their time underground and mainly eat eggs.

People have brought new plants and animals to the desert. Tumbleweeds came from Russia. They now grow as weeds in the Mojave Desert.

After the Mojave's winter rains, bighorn sheep get the water they need from green plants. They must eat fast in the hot summer, when mountain lions wait for them near water holes.

31

Words to Know

bacteria - tiny living things that help break down dead plants and animals. Bacteria can only be seen with a microscope.

carnivore - an animal that eats another animal.

decomposers - tiny living things that live on the dead remains of plants and animals as well as animal waste.

energy - power needed to work or live.

herbivore - an animal that eats plants.

nocturnal - active at night.

nutrients - chemicals that plants and animals need to live.

omnivore - an animal that eats plants and animals.

top carnivore - a carnivore that is not preyed on by other carnivores.

On the Web

To learn more about desert food chains, visit ABDO Group online at **www.abdopublishing.com**. Web sites about desert food chains are featured on our Book Links page. These links are routinely monitored and updated to provide the most current information available.

Index